BALD EAGLES

Written By: Anna DiGilio

All rights reserved. No part of this publication may be reproduced, distributed, or transmitted in any form or by any means, including photocopying, recording, or other electronic or mechanical methods, without the prior written permission of the publisher, except in the case of brief quotations embodied in critical reviews and certain other noncommercial uses permitted by copyright law.

For permission requests, write to the publisher:
Laprea Publishing
info@lapreapublishing.com

Website: www.GuidedReaders.com

ISBN: 978-1-63647-521-9

© 2021 Anna DiGilio

Photo Credits:
Cover, Title Page: Shutterstock; Brian E Kushner. 3: Shutterstock; Patthana Nirangkul. 4: Shutterstock; Jennifer Yakey-Ault. 5: Shutterstock; Ritterbiz. 6 (inset): Adobe Stock; Sebastian Bayer. 6: Shutterstock; Brian E Kushner. 7: Shutterstock; Keith 316. 8: Shutterstock; Ad_hominem. 9 (top): Shutterstock; Anakin Fox. 9 (bottom): Shutterstock; Manamana. 10: Shutterstock; Alexander Zavadsky. 11: Shutterstock; PlainJane33. 12: Wikipedia; Xanthis. 13: Adobe Stock; Krista. 14: Shutterstock; FloridaStock.

TABLE OF CONTENTS

Big Birds .... Page 4

What Bald Eagles Eat .... Page 6

Where Bald Eagles Live .... Page 8

Important Birds .... Page 10

Saving Bald Eagles .... Page 11

Flying Free .... Page 14

Glossary .... Page 15

Big Birds

Bald eagles are birds. They are big. They have many brown feathers. They have some white feathers. They have a white head. They have a white tail.

Bald eagles have big wings. They fly high in the sky. They have good eyes. They can see far.

What Bald Eagles Eat

Bald eagles eat meat. They have sharp <u>claws</u>. They catch animals with their claws. They have a sharp <u>beak</u>. They eat animals with their sharp beaks.

Bald eagle claw

A bald eagle flies down to catch a fish.

Bald eagles sit in high places. They watch for animals. They eat fish. They eat rabbits. They eat squirrels. They eat ducks. They eat geese.

A bald eagle looks for animals to eat.

Where Bald Eagles Live

Bald eagles live in the United States. Many live in Canada. Some live in Mexico.

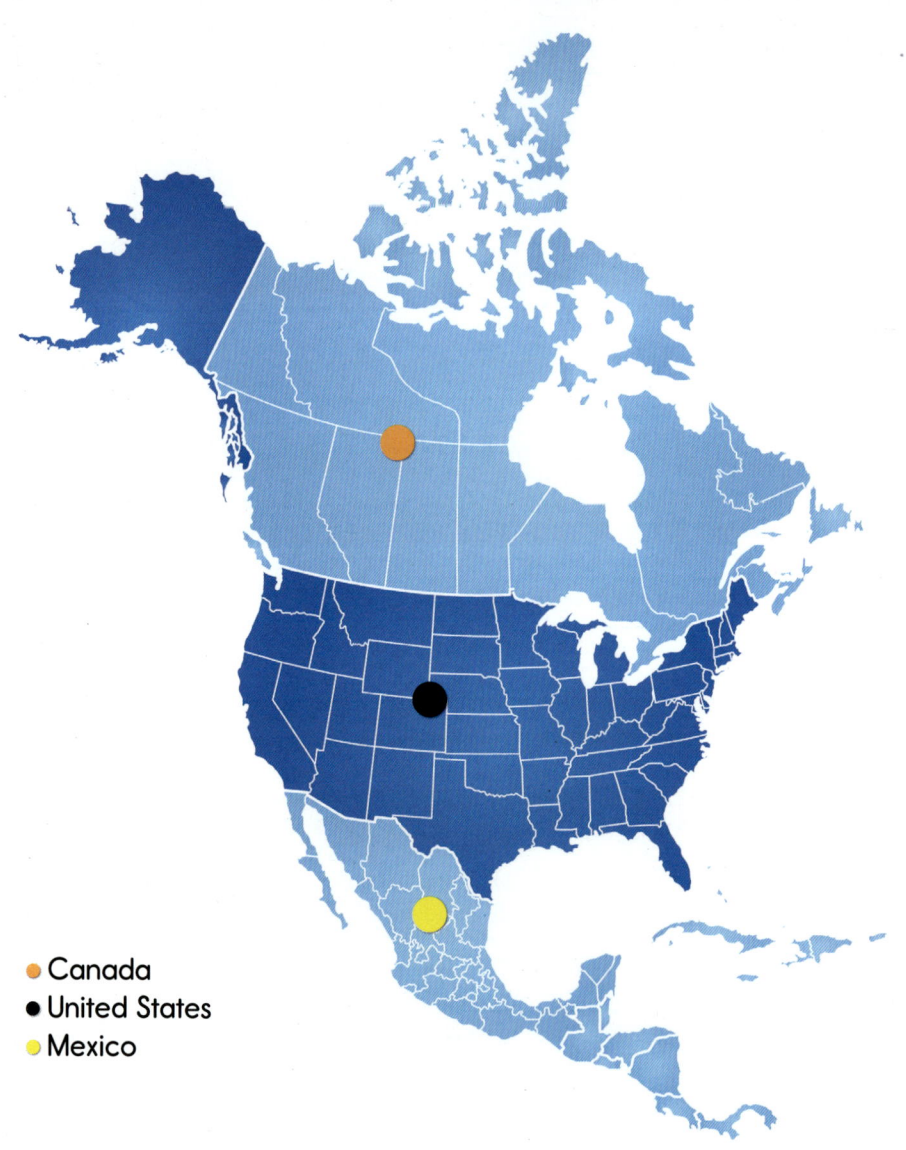

- Canada
- United States
- Mexico

Bald eagles live near water. They live near lakes. They live near rivers. They live near beaches.

Important Birds

Bald eagles are important to the United States. They are on money. They are on state flags. They are on many things.

Great Seal of the United States

Saving Bald Eagles

Long ago, people in the United States used DDT. DDT kills bugs. But DDT hurt bald eagles, too. It hurt bald eagle eggs. The shells were thin. They broke when a parent sat on them. The eggs did not <u>hatch</u>.

Bald eagle numbers <u>dropped</u>. Bald eagles almost died out. People wanted to help. They got laws changed. One law got rid of DDT. Other laws helped keep bald eagles safe.

People worked hard. Some people <u>raised</u> bald eagles. Later, they set bald eagles free. People saved bald eagles!

Flying Free

Bald eagles are big. Bald eagles are beautiful. Bald eagles are important. Fly high, bald eagles!

GLOSSARY

<u>beak</u>
the hard, sharp parts that cover the mouth of a bird, turtle, or certain other animals

<u>claws</u>
hard, curved parts at the ends of the toes of some animals

<u>dropped</u>
got lower or fewer

<u>hatch</u>
to break open when a chick or other baby animal is born

<u>raised</u>
cared for a young animal and helped it grow